Match the

bat   cat   hat

MW00963577

Write the word that matches each picture.

1. _____

4.  _____

2. _____

5.  _____

3. _____

6.  _____

Find and circle the words in the puzzle.
The words go ➜ and ↓.

m	i	r	c	t	b	c	a	t
a	h	x	s	a	t	e	b	f
t	a	v	u	i	g	x	a	o
j	t	q	r	a	t	j	t	x

All Mixed-Up

can	fan	man	pan	tan	van

Unscramble the letters. Write the words on the lines. Draw a line from each word to its picture.

1. | a | n | m | ------------------------------

2. | n | a | c | ------------------------------

3. | a | n | p | ------------------------------

4. | f | n | a | ------------------------------

5. | t | n | a | ------------------------------

6. | n | a | v | ------------------------------

FS111150 Spelling

Make a Word

| cap | lap | map | nap | sap | tap |

Write the beginning letter of each picture in the boxes to make a new word.

1. | | | |

2. | | | |

3. | | | |

4. | | | |

5. | | | |

6. | | | |

Find the Words

tag	sag	nag	wag	rag	bag

Write the words in alphabetical order.

1. _____

2. _____

3. _____

4. _____

5. _____

6. _____

Find and circle the words in the puzzle. The words go → and ↓.

x	r	a	g	b	d
w	h	e	f	c	t
a	g	i	k	m	a
g	b	a	g	j	g
z	x	l	p	r	t
s	y	x	n	n	q
a	r	o	x	a	w
g	s	t	u	g	v

4

FS111150 Spelling

How Does It End?

band	bang	hand	hang	sand	sang

Circle the correct word to complete the sentence. Write the word.

1. I have five fingers on my _____ .
   (hang, hand)

2. Please _____ up your coat.
   (hang, hand)

3. The _____ played a song.
   (band, bang)

4. He shut the door with a _____ .
   (band, bang)

5. We played in the _____ .
   (sang, sand)

6. The bird _____ in the trees.
   (sang, sand)

FS111150 Spelling

Finish the Sentences

Ben   den   hen

men   pen   ten

Write the correct word to finish each sentence.

1. Some wild animals live in a _____ .

2. The _____ laid many eggs.

3. May I borrow your blue _____ ?

4. The number after nine is _____ .

My name is Ben.

5. His first name is _____ .

6. Two _____ are sitting on the bench.

FS111150 Spelling

It Begins Like . . .

get	let	met	net	pet	wet

Write the word that answers each question.

1. What word begins like ?

_____

2. What word begins like ?

_____

3. What word begins like ?

_____

4. What word begins like ?

_____

5. What word begins like ?

_____

6. What word begins like ?

_____

FS111150 Spelling

Hidden Words

bed   fed   led

red   Ted   wed

Find and circle the hidden word in each set of letters. Write the words.

1. r e x r e d q   _____

2. x b e d e p o   _____

3. e c z T e d d   _____

4. e d l l e d s   _____

5. b v f e d k m   _____

6. w e d k a a d   _____

What's in the Tent?

| bend | lend | send | dent | tent | went |

Write each word on the correct tent.

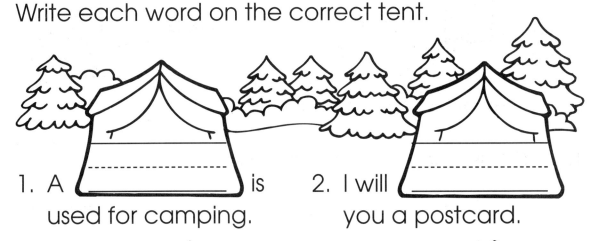

1. A _____ is used for camping.

2. I will _____ you a postcard.

3. I will _____ down and tie my shoe.

4. I will _____ you my pencil.

5. The _____ in the car is small.

6. I _____ to bed early last night.

FS111150 Spelling

It's Misspelled

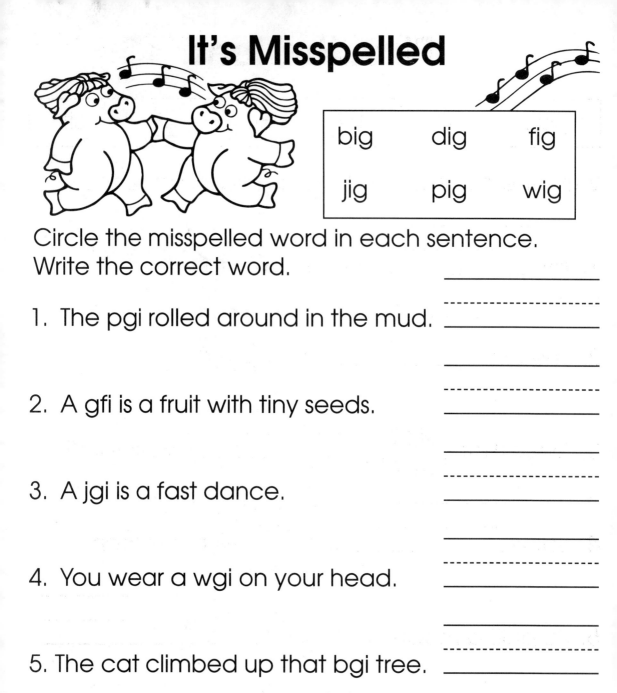

big	dig	fig
jig	pig	wig

Circle the misspelled word in each sentence.
Write the correct word.

_____
1. The pgi rolled around in the mud.   _____

_____
2. A gfi is a fruit with tiny seeds.   _____

_____
3. A jgi is a fast dance.   _____

_____
4. You wear a wgi on your head.   _____

_____
5. The cat climbed up that bgi tree.   _____

_____
6. The men had to gdi a large hole.   _____

Picture Clues

bit	fit	hit	kit	lit	sit

Write the correct word to finish each sentence.

1. He _____ the ball with the  .

2. The girl _____ the .

3. Does that  _____ your foot?

4. Jack _____ the with a match.

5. Jo built a model from a _____ .

6. Chickens _____ on their  .

FS111150 Spelling

Which Word?

Circle the correct word to complete the sentence. Write the word.

in	bin	fin
pin	tin	win

1. Do you have a safety _____ ?
   (win, pin, tin)

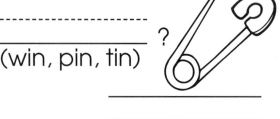

2. You can store things in a _____ .
   (bin, in, pin)

3. Did Sam _____ the race?
   (fin, win, tin)

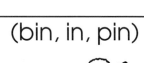

4. A fish has more than one _____ .
   (win, in, fin)

5. Patrick threw away the _____ can.
   (tin, in, win)

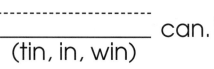

6. Did the cat go _____ the house?
   (bin, in, fin)

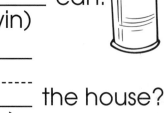

Fishing for Words

king	ring	sing	hint	mint	tint

Color the words that end with **nt** blue.
Color the words that end with **ng** yellow.

tint

king

ring

sing

mint

hint

Write the three words that end with **nt**.

_____   _____   _____

Write the three words that end with **ng**.

_____   _____   _____

Finish It!

dot	got	hot	lot	not	pot

Look at the pictures. Complete the sentences.

 1. What a _____ day!

 2. There are a _____ of stars.

 3. The dog is _____ in the house.

 4. The plant is in the _____ .

 5. He made a _____ with his pen.

 6. She _____ a new car.

 FS111150 Spelling

Searching for Words

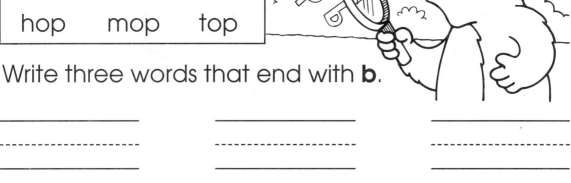

job	rob	sob
hop	mop	top

Write three words that end with **b**.

_____   _____   _____
-------------   -------------   -------------
_____   _____   _____

Write three words that end with **p**.

_____   _____   _____
-------------   -------------   -------------
_____   _____   _____

Find and circle the words in the puzzle.
The words go ➡ and ⬇.

x	h	o	p	a	x	d	j	t	n	s
r	f	o	s	o	p	x	o	o	m	o
o	r	k	b	j	o	b	p	b	o	b
p	o	m	t	o	p	w	q	x	u	v
g	b	l	c	s	t	m	o	p	e	r

Figure It Out!

dog	hog	jog	box	fox	ox

Unscramble the letters. Write the words correctly.

_____   _____   _____

- - - - - - - - - - -   - - - - - - - - - - -   - - - - - - - - - - -

gdo   oxf   jgo

_____   _____   _____

- - - - - - - - - - -   - - - - - - - - - - -   - - - - - - - - - - -

xo   gho   xob

Look at the pictures. Write the words.

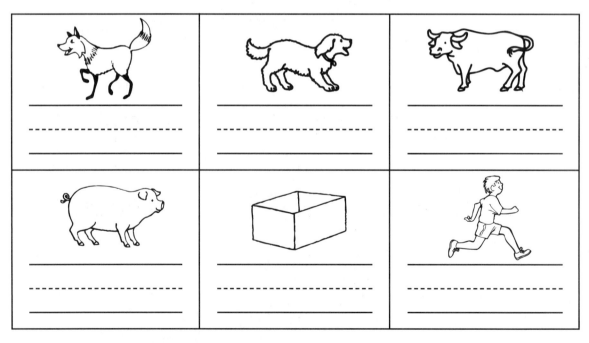

A Sock on a Rock

lock   rock   sock

bond   fond   pond

Unscramble the letters.
Write the word that fits in each sentence.

1. (kcol) Did you _____ the door?

2. (ndop) A _____ is smaller than a lake.

3. (bdon) Glue can _____ things together.

4. (rkoc) I found a shiny _____ at the lake.

5. (donf) I am very _____ of animals.

6. (skoc) I lost a _____ .

What's in the Bug?

bug   dug   hug   jug   mug   rug

Find and circle the hidden word in each bug.
Write the words.

1.  b u j u g x _____

2.  m u g u n w _____

3.  a p u d u g _____

4.  c h u g h p _____

5. z u b u g v _____

6. r u j r u g _____

FS111150 Spelling

Having Fun

bun	fun	pun	run	sun

Circle the correct word to complete the
sentence. Write the word.

1. We had _____ on the ride.
   (bun, pun, fun)

2. Bill had to _____ to get to school.
   (sun, run, bun)

3. A hamburger has a _____ .
   (fun, bun, run)

4. A _____ is a kind of joke.
   (sun, run, pun)

5. The _____ gives light and heat.
   (sun, bun, pun)

Scrambled P's and T's

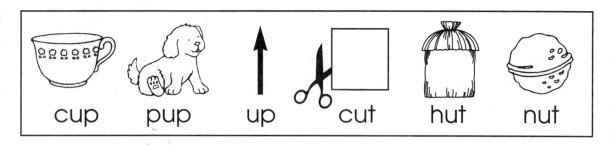

cup   pup   up   cut   hut   nut

Write three words that end with **p**.

_____

_____

_____

Write three words that end with **t**.

_____

_____

_____

Unscramble the letters. Write the words correctly.

_____
pu

_____
pcu

_____
utc

_____
htu

_____
ppu

_____
tun

Jump for Joy

duck	luck	tuck	bump	jump	pump

Find and circle the words in the puzzle.
The words go ➔ and ↓.

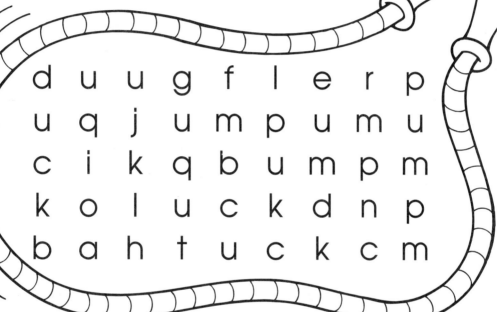

```
d u u g f l e r p
u q j u m p u m u
c i k q b u m p m
k o l u c k d n p
b a h t u c k c m
```

Finish the words below.

1.

2.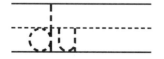

3.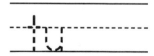

4.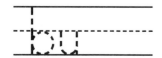

5.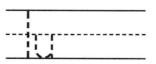

6.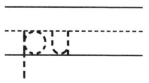

FS111150 Spelling

Using Clues

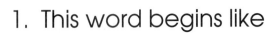

| date | fate | gate | hate | late | mate |

Read the clues. Then write the words.

1. This word begins like  . _____

2. This word begins like  . _____

3. This word begins like  . _____

4. This word begins like . _____

5. This word begins like  . _____

6. This word begins like  . _____

FS111150 Spelling

Tasty Cakes

bake   cake   lake   rake   take   wake

Write each word on the correct piece of cake.

1. I ate a piece of _____.

2. Let's _____ a walk.

3. Don't _____ the baby!

4. Did you _____ the leaves?

5. Let's fish at the _____.

6. People _____ things in ovens.

Crossword Fun

fade	made	came
game	name	same

Read the clues.
Write the words
in the puzzle.

Down

1. The twins are wearing the _____ outfit.
2. He _____ to the party last night.
3. Her first _____ is Jessica.

Across

4. I _____ a birthday card for my mom.
5. Let's play that _____ again.
6. Did the color _____ ?

Picture Perfect

be	he	me	she	we

Look at the picture.
Underline the correct sentence.

1. **He** has a dog.

   She has a dog.

2. **He** is playing.

   We are playing.

3. She will **be** a clown.

   We are clowns.

4. **She** has a hat.

   He has a hat.

5. Mom gave **me** a hug.

   We gave Mom a card.

Finish the Words

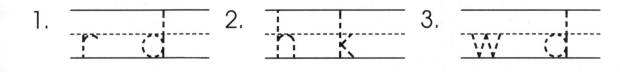

hide   ride   wide   bike   hike   like

Finish the words below.

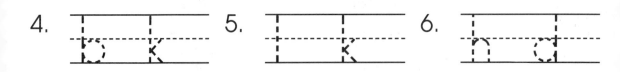

1. r _ d   2. h _ k   3. w _ d

4. b _ k   5. _ _ k   6. h _ d

Find and circle the words in the puzzle.
The words go → and ↓.

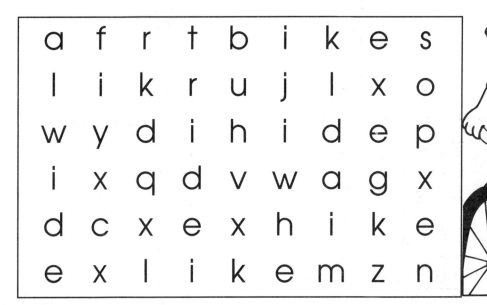

a	f	r	t	b	i	k	e	s
l	i	k	r	u	j	l	x	o
w	y	d	i	h	i	d	e	p
i	x	q	d	v	w	a	g	x
d	c	x	e	x	h	i	k	e
e	x	l	i	k	e	m	z	n

Pull-Out Answers

Page 1
1. cat
2. hat
3. mat
4. sat
5. bat
6. rat

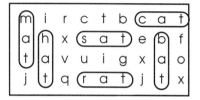

Page 2
1. man
2. can
3. pan
4. fan
5. tan
6. van

Page 3
1. sap
2. cap
3. nap
4. lap
5. tap
6. map

Page 4
1. bag
2. nag
3. rag
4. sag
5. tag
6. wag

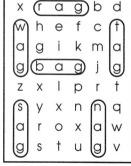

Page 5
1. hand
2. hang
3. band
4. bang
5. sand
6. sang

Page 6
1. den
2. hen
3. pen
4. ten
5. Ben
6. men

Page 7
1. pet
2. met
3. let
4. get
5. wet
6. net

Page 8
1. red
2. bed
3. Ted
4. led
5. fed
6. wed

Page 9
1. tent
2. send
3. bend
4. lend
5. dent
6. went

Page 10
1. circled—pgi
   written—pig
2. circled—gfi
   written—fig
3. circled—jgi
   written—jig
4. circled—wgi
   written—wig
5. circled—bgi
   written—big
6. circled—gdi
   written—dig

Page 11
1. hit
2. bit
3. fit
4. lit
5. kit
6. sit

Page 12
1. pin
2. bin
3. win
4. fin
5. tin
6. in

Page 13
blue: hint, mint, tint
yellow: king, ring, sing

hint, mint, tint;
king, ring, sing

Page 14
1. hot
2. lot
3. not
4. pot
5. dot
6. got

A

FS111150 Spelling

Pull-Out Answers

Page 15
job, rob, sob;
hop, mop, top

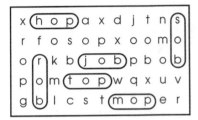

Page 16
dog, fox, jog;
ox, hog, box

fox, dog ox;
hog, box, jog

Page 17
1. lock
2. pond
3. bond
4. rock
5. fond
6. sock

Page 18
1. jug
2. mug
3. dug
4. hug
5. bug
6. rug

Page 19
1. fun
2. run
3. bun
4. pun
5. sun

Page 20
cup
pup
up

cut
hut
nut

up, cup, cut;
hut, pup, nut

Page 21

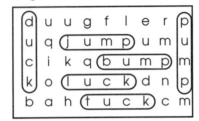

1. jump
2. duck
3. tuck
4. bump
5. luck
6. pump

Page 22
1. gate
2. mate
3. fate
4. late
5. date
6. hate

Page 23
1. cake
2. take
3. wake
4. rake
5. lake
6. bake

Page 24

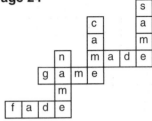

Page 25
1. **He** has a dog.
2. **We** are playing.
3. She will **be** a clown.
4. **She** has a hat.
5. Mom gave **me** a hug.

Page 26
1. ride
2. hike
3. wide
4. bike
5. like
6. hide

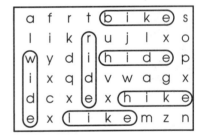

Page 27
1. five
2. lime
3. dime
4. hive
5. dive
6. time

lime, dive, five;
time, hive, dime

Pull-Out Answers

Page 28

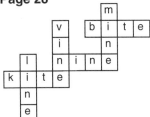

Page 29
1. circled—rpoe
   written—rope
2. circled—onte
   written—tone
3. circled—pohe
   written—hope
4. circled—oneb
   written—bone
5. circled—neoc
   written—cone
6. circled—onze
   written—zone

Page 30
1. hole
2. rose
3. pole
4. mole
5. hose
6. nose

Page 31
1. use
2. tune
3. fuse
4. mule
5. rule
6. dune

Page 32
1. shape
2. shine
3. shed
4. ship
5. shut
6. shop

Page 33
1. chop
2. chin
3. chip
4. chat
5. chime
6. check

Page 34
1. this
2. those
3. these
4. that
5. them
6. then

Page 35
1. when
2. which
3. whole
4. whale
5. whip
6. while

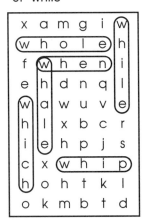

Page 36
1. clap
2. blend
3. block
4. clip
5. club
6. blimp

Page 37
1. flag
2. glue
3. flute
4. glad
5. flat
6. globe

Page 38
1. plug
2. sled
3. slip
4. plate
5. plum
6. slide

Page 39

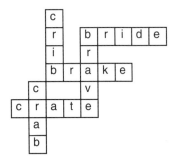

Page 40
1. drive
2. frame
3. froze
4. drip
5. frog
6. drop

FS111150 Spelling

Pull-Out Answers

Page 41

grin
grip
grape

trade
trap
trip

Page 42
mail
drain
nail
rain
train
tail

Page 43
1. clay
2. bay
3. tray
4. play
5. hay
6. stay

Page 44
1. meet
2. seed
3. keep
4. feet
5. need
6. week

Page 45
1. cry
2. fly
3. sky
4. by
5. my
6. why

Page 46
1. to
2. and
3. is
4. do
5. are
6. of

Page 47
1. from
2. said
3. you
4. come
5. have
6. who

Page 48
1. some
2. has
3. will
4. our
5. were
6. there

Page 49
1. yellow
2. red
3. orange
4. black
5. blue
6. white
7. brown
8. green

Page 50
1. three
2. five
3. seven
4. one
5. nine
6. two
7. four
8. ten
9. six
10. eight

Page 51
1. girl
2. father
3. boy
4. sister
5. mother
6. brother

Page 52
1. cat
2. sing
3. jump
4. game
5. cone
6. check
7. week

FS111150 Spelling

Time to Spell

dime	lime	time	dive	five	hive

Write the word that matches each picture.

1. **5** _____

4. 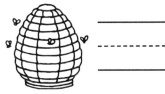 _____

2. _____

5. _____

3. _____

6.  _____

Unscramble the letters. Write the words correctly.

_____
mile

_____
vied

_____
vefi

_____
tmei

_____
heiv

_____
dmie

More Crossword Fun

Read the clues. Write the words in the puzzle.

bite	kite	line
mine	nine	vine

Across

3. I took a _____ of that candy bar.
5. The number after eight is _____ .
6. I like to fly a _____ .

Down

1. That book is not yours, it's _____ .
2. A _____ is a plant with a long, thin stem.
4. We stood in a long _____ .

Spell It Right

| hope | rope | bone | cone | tone | zone |

Circle the misspelled word in each sentence.
Write the correct word.

1. Do you like to jump rpoe?

   _____

   _____

2. She used an angry onte of voice.

   _____

   _____

3. I pohe it snows tomorrow!

   _____

   _____

4. The dog buried its oneb.

   _____

   _____

5. I like to eat ice cream in a neoc.

   _____

   _____

6. Drive safely in a school onze.

   _____

   _____

Write It Right

hole	mole	pole	hose	nose	rose

Unscramble the letters. Write the words on the lines. Draw a line from each word to its picture.

1. olhe

_____

_____

4. mloe

_____

_____

2. rseo

_____

_____

5. ehso

_____

_____

3. eolp

_____

_____

6. noes

_____

_____

Letter Math

mule	rule	dune	tune	fuse	use

Follow the signs. Add and subtract the letters.
Write the words.

1. usage – ag = _____

2. tuna – a + e = _____

3. fun – n + se = _____

4. mug – g + let – t = _____

5. run – n + l + e = _____

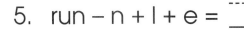

6. dug – g + ne = _____

FS111150 Spelling

Which Picture?

shape   shed   shine   ship   shop   shut

Complete the words below.
Circle the correct picture.

1.	sha___e	
2.	shi___e	
3.	she___	
4.	shi___	
5.	shu___	
6.	sho___	

Change a Letter

Change one letter in each word to make a word from the list. Then draw a line to match each word to its picture.

chat	check
chin	chip
chime	chop

1. shop
_____

2. thin
_____

3. ship
_____

4. that
_____

5. chimp
_____

6. cheek
_____

FS111150 Spelling

This or That?

that	them	then
these	this	those

Write the correct word to finish each sentence.

1. That dog is smaller than _____ one.

2. Did you see _____ clowns over there?

3. Do you like _____ shoes I'm wearing?

4. Do you want this toy or _____ one?

5. We picked _____ up at the airport.

6. First we ate and _____ we played.

FS111150 Spelling

Which Word?

Write the word that rhymes with each picture.

whale	when	which
while	whip	whole

1.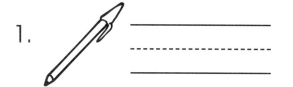

Find and circle the words in the puzzle. The words go → and ↓.

2.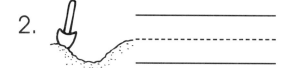

3.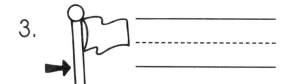

x	a	m	g	i	w
w	h	o	l	e	h
f	w	h	e	n	i
e	h	d	n	q	l
w	a	w	u	v	e
h	l	x	b	c	r
i	e	h	p	j	s
c	x	w	h	i	p
h	o	h	t	k	l
o	k	m	b	t	d

4.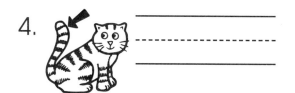

5.

6.

Crack the Code

blend   blimp   block   clap   clip   club

Use the code to figure out the words.

❖	= a
▲	= b
◆	= c
✓	= d
✕	= e
■	= i
●	= k
▼	= l
★	= m
✚	= n
✳	= o
♥	= p
→	= u

1. ◆ ▼ ❖ ♥ _____

2. ▲ ▼ ✕ ✚ ✓ _____

3. ▲ ▼ ✳ ◆ ● _____

4. ◆ ▼ ■ ♥ _____

5. ◆ ▼ → ▲ _____

6. ▲ ▼ ■ ★ ♥ _____

FS111150 Spelling

What Shape?

| flag | flat | flute | glad | globe | glue |

Write each word in the correct word shape.

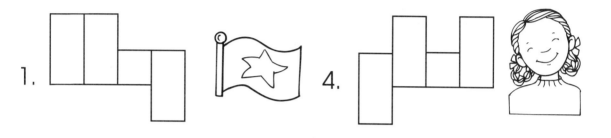

1.

4.

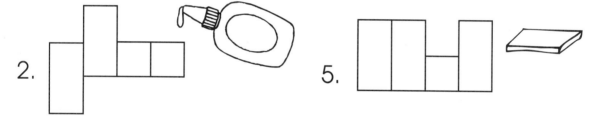

2.

5.

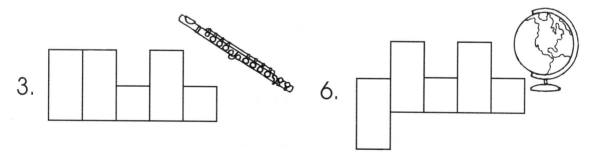

3.

6.

FS111150 Spelling

Adding Letters

plate	plum	plug	sled	slide	slip

Add the letters. Write the word.
Circle the correct picture.

1. pl + ug = _____

2. sl + ed = _____

3. sl + ip = _____

4. pl + ate = _____

5. pl + um = _____

6. sl + ide = _____

FS111150 Spelling

Lots of Clues

Read the clues.
Write the words
in the puzzle.

brake

brave

bride

crab

crate

crib

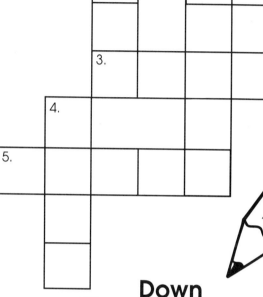

Across

2. The _____ wore a white gown.

3. The _____ is used to stop a wheel.

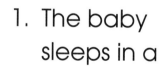

5. The oranges were in a _____ .

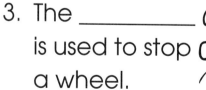

Down

1. The baby sleeps in a _____ .

2. The _____ soldier was not afraid.

4. A _____ lives in the water.

Drip or Drop?

drip	drive	drop	frame	frog	froze

Look at the pictures. Complete the sentences.

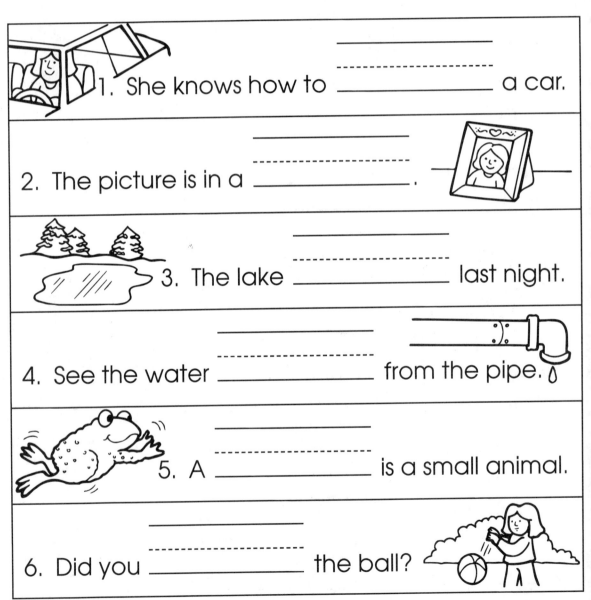

1. She knows how to _____ a car.

2. The picture is in a _____ .

3. The lake _____ last night.

4. See the water _____ from the pipe.

5. A _____ is a small animal.

6. Did you _____ the ball?

FS111150 Spelling

Across and Down

grin	grip	grape
trade	trap	trip

Find and circle the words in the puzzle. The words go → and ↓.

Write three words that begin with **gr**.

_____
- - - - - - - - - - - - - -
_____
- - - - - - - - - - - - - -
_____
- - - - - - - - - - - - - -
_____

r	a	b	g	a	f	q
h	t	r	a	d	e	p
d	r	h	e	i	m	j
s	a	t	z	y	o	k
o	b	g	r	i	n	l
g	x	r	b	w	f	t
r	u	i	c	i	m	r
a	c	p	d	e	g	i
p	v	x	t	r	a	p
e	n	l	d	j	k	n

Write three words that begin with **tr**.

_____
- - - - - - - - - - - - - -
_____
- - - - - - - - - - - - - -
_____
- - - - - - - - - - - - - -
_____

Make a Match

drain   mail   nail   rain   tail   train

Unscramble the letters. Write the words on the lines. Draw a line from the picture to its word.

- lmai ----------------------------

- nrdai ----------------------------

- ianl ----------------------------

- rnia ----------------------------

- nrtia ----------------------------

- liat ----------------------------

FS111150 Spelling

Sound Alikes

bay   clay   hay   play   stay   tray

Write the word that answers each question.

1. What word begins like  ? _____

2. What word begins like ? _____

3. What word begins like ? _____

4. What word begins like  ? _____

5. What word begins like ? _____

6. What word begins like ? _____

Super Seeds

| need | seed | week | keep | feet | meet |

Complete the sentences.

1. Please _____ me at nine o'clock.

2. A _____ is a part of a plant.

3. Can I _____ this picture?

4. My _____ are tired from walking.

5. I _____ to take a break.

6. A _____ has seven days.

Please Don't Cry

by	cry	fly	my	sky	why

Follow the signs. Add and subtract the letters.
Write the words.

1. crab – ab + y = _____

2. flag – ag + y = _____

3. skip – ip + y = _____

4. big – ig + y = _____

5. man – an + y = _____

6. whip – ip + y = _____

High Frequency Words

and	are	do	is	of	to

Use the code to figure out the words.

● = a	■ = f	✶ = n	✧ = s
▲ = d	★ = h	✖ = o	❖ = t
◆ = e	♥ = i	♠ = r	✚ = u

1. ❖ ✖
_____

2. ● ✶ ▲
_____

3. ♥ ✧
_____

4. ▲ ✖
_____

5. ● ♠ ◆
_____

6. ✖ ■
_____

FS111150 Spelling

Look at the Shapes

come	from	have
said	who	you

Write each word in the correct word shape.

1. I got a letter ⬚⬚⬚⬚ my grandma.

2. She ⬚⬚⬚⬚ good-bye to everyone.

3. Do ⬚⬚⬚ like ice cream?

4. Patrick will ⬚⬚⬚⬚ to the party.

5. I ⬚⬚⬚⬚ to clean my room now.

6. Do you know ⬚⬚⬚ wrote that book?

FS111150 Spelling

Mystery Words

has	our	some	there	were	will

Use the code to figure out the words.

a	b	c	d	e	f	g	h	i	j	k	l	m
1	2	3	4	5	6	7	8	9	10	11	12	13

n	o	p	q	r	s	t	u	v	w	x	y	z
14	15	16	17	18	19	20	21	22	23	24	25	26

1. ___ ___ ___ ___
   19 15 13 5

2. ___ ___ ___
   8 1 19

3. ___ ___ ___ ___
   23 9 12 12

4. ___ ___ ___
   15 21 18

5. ___ ___ ___ ___
   23 5 18 5

6. ___ ___ ___ ___ ___
   20 8 5 18 5

What Color?

black	blue	brown	green
orange	red	white	yellow

Complete the words below. Color the pictures.

1. ye_____

2. r_____

3. or_____

4. _____ck

5. _____ue

6. _____te

7. br_____

8. gr_____

Number Words

one	two	three	four	five
six	seven	eight	nine	ten

Count. Write the number word.

1. _____

6. _____

2. _____

7. _____

3. _____

8. _____

4. _____

9. _____

5. _____

10. _____

FS111150 Spelling

Family Words

| boy | girl | brother | sister | father | mother |

Add the letters. Write the word.
Circle the correct picture.

1. gi + rl = _____

2. fath + er = _____

3. b + oy = _____

4. sis + ter = _____

5. mo + ther = _____

6. bro + ther = _____

FS111150 Spelling

Spelling Review

The boldfaced words are misspelled.
Fill in the bubbles to show the
correct spelling of each word.

1. The **cta** likes to chase mice.
   - ◯ tac
   - ◯ cat
   - ◯ act

2. Do you want to **nisg** a song?
   - ◯ gins
   - ◯ sgin
   - ◯ sing

3. It's fun to **jpum** rope.
   - ◯ jump
   - ◯ jmup
   - ◯ upjm

4. Checkers is a fun **geam.**
   - ◯ mage
   - ◯ game
   - ◯ gema

5. Tim ate an ice cream **cnoe.**
   - ◯ noec
   - ◯ ceon
   - ◯ cone

6. The teacher made a **ckech** on my paper.
   - ◯ check
   - ◯ ckche
   - ◯ ckche

7. There are seven days in a **keew**.
   - ◯ weke
   - ◯ week
   - ◯ eekw